The Water Age

And Other Fictions

Tracey Warr

MEANDA BOOKS

Meanda Books
https://meandabooks.com

Cover by James A. Hudson

Book Layout © 2017 BookDesignTemplates.com

The Water Age #1: The Water Age and Other Fictions/ Tracey Warr. -- 1st ed.
ISBN 978-0-9954902-1-5

The Water Age Series

The Water Age and Other Fictions (#1)
The Water Age Art and Writing Workshops (#2)
The Water Age Children's Art and Writing Workshops (#3)

The Water Age is a series of three books by Tracey Warr. The books contemplate water and futures through fiction and through art and writing workshops. The books were produced as part of the *Frontiers in Retreat* project. They were co-produced by HIAP, with the support of the EU Culture Programme.

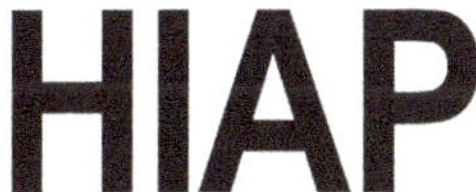 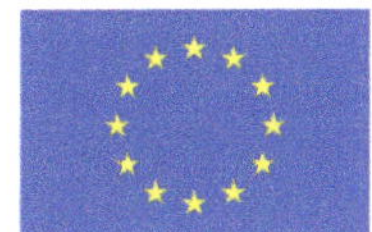

This project has been funded with support from the European Commission. This publication reflects the views only of the author, and the Commission cannot be held responsible for any use which may be made of the information contained therein.

CONTENTS

Earth's Lament   1

Meanda   5

The Extraterrestrial   37

FORD   41

The Water Age   53

Asbrú   55

Notes   65

Thanks   69

Earth's Lament

Of things I'd rather keep in silence I must sing
so bitter do I feel toward you
whom I love more than anything.

You left me for another planet,
my forests silent, my seas emptied.
Come home now. I have healed the scars you graved.

It's not right another celestial body takes you away from me.
Remember how it was with us in the beginning!
Come home. We could still have much time together
Before the death throes of the sun begin.

I send you there, on your exoplanet,
this song as messenger and delegate.
Come home my lovers, my humans.

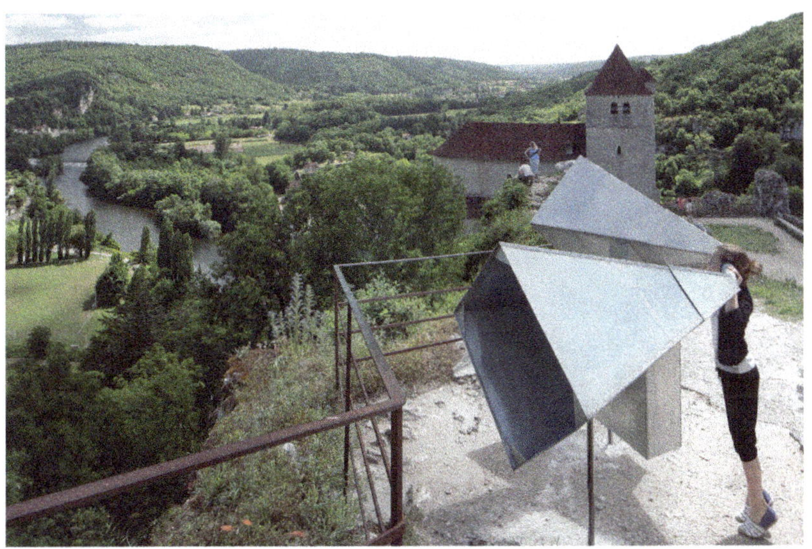

Tania Candiani, *Landscape Sound Amplifier*, 2016. Site specific installation above the River Lot in Saint Cirq Lapopie, France, in the *Exoplanet Lot* exhibition organised by Maison des Arts Georges et Claude Pompidou. Courtesy of the artist. Photo by Yohann Gozard. 'Earth's Lament' was originally written to be heard through this sculpture.

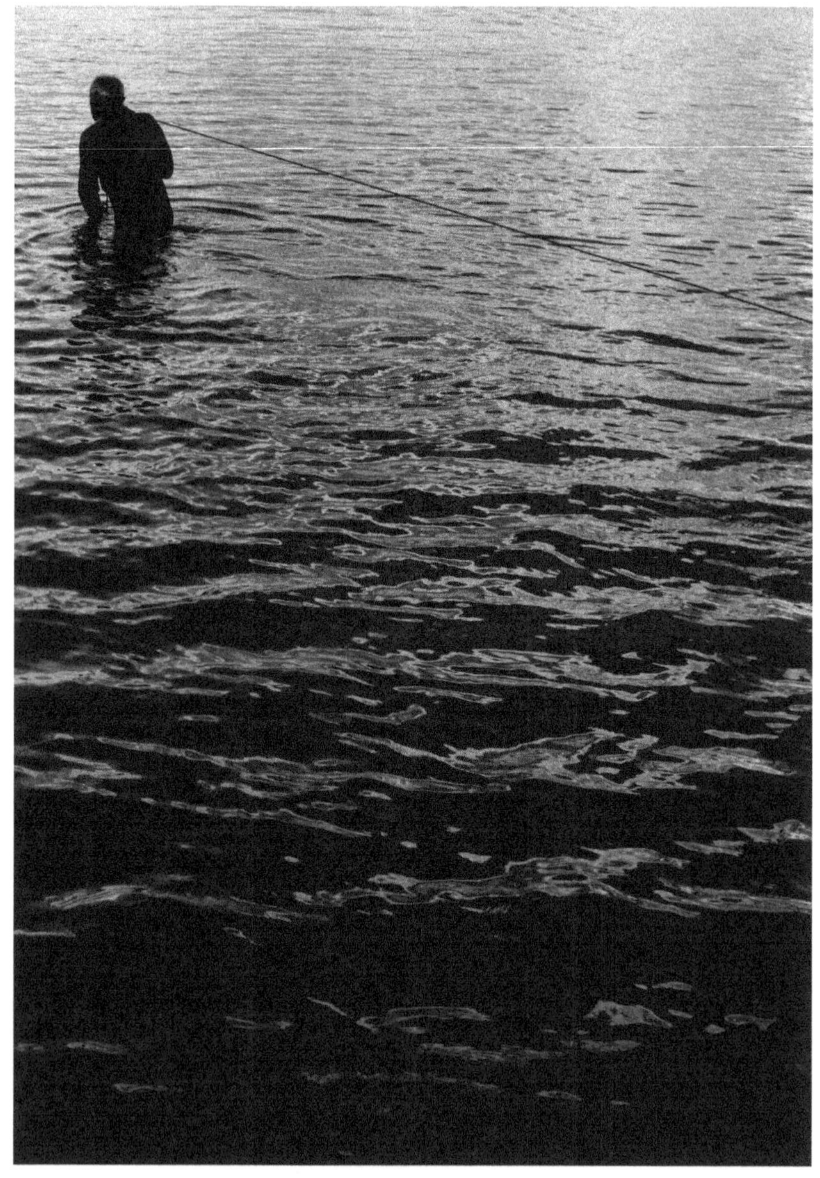

Photo by James A. Hudson.

Meanda

The water moved her silently through the purple lily patch to-wards the river bank, where she could get a better view of the white sphere.

Frank, the expedition artist, wrote in his journal:

Took first steps on exoplanet Kepler-55555b. Made hasty sketches. Planet covered in oceans, rivers, archipelagos, teeming with aquatic life. Swung round when I heard something big in the water near a patch of lilies but missed sight of it. Robo-fish probes will find out more about what is in the water.

Settlement planning for Murdon and the other 'Wealths' begins tomorrow. Captain Lena has decided to terraform the islands into larger landmasses and discipline the rivers. The thrill of a blank canvas, an empty planet to do better with. Projections give Earth only fifty more years. It's grotesquely ugly back home and will get a lot worse.

Real environmental costing was introduced way too late to do any good, to counter the impacts of ice-melts, sea-rises, mutating micropollutants in the water. Wracking to get pure water out of the serpentine, the wet rocks in Earth's mantle hundreds of miles down, worked for a while until chasms opened up swallowing buildings, whole villages. The 'Wealths' are still lining their pockets through everyone else's distress. They need those pockets well-lined too, not to rescue their fellow humans, but to save themselves, to pay for their exoplanet escape. Capitalism is cannibalism.

Frank doodled the last full stop, enlarging it until it looked like a small planet. Maybe he should go awol on Kepler-55555b instead of returning to the degraded and doomed environment of Earth, as his contract insisted.

Morning water rose as mist twisting around itself, receiving the heat of the new day, evaporating to drift in darkening clouds, or meandered sluggishly in the river, loaded with dissolved soil and vegetation, or light with oxygen and frivolity. Further to the north, water bloomed viscous, turning to ice, forming delicate snowflakes or bludgeoning shards of hail. Water geysered high into the air, thundered in sheer, glassy sheets down high rock-faces.

Frank and Lena started out exploring together, marvelling at the river's incised meander that wound past honey-coloured lofty cliffs and dark cave openings. Vines covered the sunny slopes and a tangle of rich vegetation flourished on the plains. The weather sped through extremes. At an intensely green rectangular pond they watched small beasts, like tiny horses, sipping at the water's edge, and dragonflies hovering above the yellow flags of irises. 'Those lakes look deliberately cut,' Frank said.

'Amazing what heavy rainfall will do!' Lena shouted above the onset of a flash storm, grabbing his hand and pulling him to the shelter of a rocky overhang. They watched the tempest, laughing like children. Frank glanced surreptitiously at her face in profile. She was attractive. But there'd be no point in it would there, with Earth's imminent demise—or perhaps that meant there was every point in it? The storm passed as rapidly as it had arrived, ceasing abruptly so that they could emerge to a rainbow and fat waterdrops hanging from glossy leaves, reflecting the world around them as microcosms.

Lena went to join the scientific survey team and Frank continued on alone, taking photographs and pushing his way deep into a wood. He noticed branches and leaves that looked like a shelter. Could they have fallen into that form naturally? A shiver ran down the back of his neck and he span around. Twigs cracked and boughs ached with the wind. Emerging on the other side of the wood he saw a semi-circular stone formation in the river. He stumbled. At his feet lay an object woven from vines and bamboo. He took a few fast photographs, feeling spooked by the deliberate making he was looking at. Swiftly, feeling ashamed of his speed, he jogged back to the ship to show his photographs to Lena and the crew.

'It's a shelter—constructed,' he said, pointing at one image, 'and this one's a fish trap in the river. The stone barrier's been built. There'll be more of these woven baskets suspended below water.'

'Just looks like fallen branches, boulders in the river and some kind of animal nest to me, Frank,' Lena said. 'There's no intelligent life-form showing up on the instrumentation. Think of bower bird nests, beaver dams, wasp nests. There are plenty of amazing animal structures.'

'Were,' Frank reminded her. 'Those species are all extinct now.'

She frowned, exasperated. 'Frank! That's by the by. You're making a meal of nothing with these photographs. Wanting to see things that just aren't there.'

A drop of water slid from Frank's hair onto the table and sat in a tiny ball, cohering. Lena reached out a hand, touching her fingertip to the water drop, momentarily flattening it, so that it spread into a miniscule pool. When she retracted her finger, it slowly began the task of reforming its sphere.

Polarised water droplets searched for the others, merging quickly into one when they touched. Water loves water.

Next day, Frank returned to the same place to sketch. He found himself adding a shadow to the edge of his drawings, sometimes an abstract patch of bluish-green, sometimes a dark, threatening grey. He wanted to draw the beauty of the life all around him and his fear that it, too, would be destroyed and lost, but The Wealths didn't want to see that: paradise lost, his vision of this pristine world overlaid with memories of what they had done on Earth. He was just producing an estate agent's brochure for their exclusive settlement.

How could he capture the variegated colours of this water? Blue, green, brown, silvery with two moons' light, streaked with flashes of turquoise bioluminescence, black with the new light of dawn, reflecting palest blue skies. Earth's water was red with algae and iron, lurid green with phosphate and sewage, choked with plastic debris.

How could he capture the diverse speeds of this water? Calm, gyring, turbulent in spate. The water surface suddenly heaved and moved against its own flow, the whole river seeming to rise up as one, crossing itself diagonally, and then subsiding with relief on the other side. He knew the movement was caused by a gust of wind, but it was impossible not to imagine it as something coming from below, something alive.

He tried to draw the architectures of the water: circle ripples of fish rising to gum an insect; the wide Vs trailing behind a pair of duck-like birds with long bright blue beaks; pillows of water leaping in front of a submerged rock; the riffles, glides and pools; static fish suspended in deep, dark, liquid pockets. Frank's wrist ached with the effort to capture vortices, organic oil slicks, the glitter paths of tiny, reflected suns. The water smelt earthy and fresh. It rocked, lapped, crashed and careered around rocks. Pale roots waved beneath the inscrutable surface. This was just a river. How was he going to cope with drawing the oceans? Because of the constantly shifting interplay of liquid, light and reflections, no drawing, photograph or film could capture the exquisite complexities of Kepler-55555b.

Frank put down his sketchbook, zipped his wetsuit, adjusted the headcam and slid into the silky water. Tresses of aquatic plants reached for him, tickling and tangling. He submerged and swam along the rock structure, looking for signs of intervention, for more of those woven fish traps. Nothing.

He came up out of the water and saw it.

Standing quite close in the water, looking directly at him. A woman. Not a woman. Fleeting glimpse of a sleek head, dark wet hair slicked over one shoulder, pale skin; eyes—an extraordinary turquoise colour—a little closer together, little higher up on the head than a human face; tiny nose and ears, flat against the head. It submerged.

Frank hauled himself onto the bank. This was it. First contact. He ran towards where he had seen it and caught sight of a dark shadow in the water, around six feet long, streamlined, one arm extended. It moved so fast, seeming to make no effort, just an occasional sinuous movement, bending, slipping with the curves of the river. He couldn't keep up. It disappeared into a murky pool and was gone.

Frank stood, hands on his knees, catching his breath. 'Hello!' he called out, straightening up, shading his eyes to scan the sparkling surface of the river and the far bank. The water blanked him.

He ran back to his gear, stripped off the wet suit, pulled on a pair of shorts. Pencil in hand, he spun on the spot, searching for his sketchbook, desperate to capture on paper what he had seen. 'What?' Frantically, he picked up and put down the few things he'd brought with him. 'No!'

They were gone: sketchbook and journal.

'Please!' he called out to the river. 'I need those books!' A hundred birds rose from the trees at the sound of his voice but nothing else responded.

Hurriedly, on a scrap of paper from his pocket, he sketched it standing in the water, then the shadow beneath the water. It had been such a vivid glimpse and yet he could give no vividness to the drawings. Frank stared, disconsolate, at the river, resolved not to tell the crew, not yet, not till he had irrefutable proof they couldn't laugh at. Or was that really his reason for keeping the swimmer to himself?

Jorunn easily lost her pursuer in the water, doubled back, swimming deep past him, and took his books. She watched him from the cover of the trees. When he left, she plugged her mycelium translator into a dangling sugary fruit. Charging would take a while. She leafed through the sketches he had made of trees, birds, fish and her broken fish-trap. She looked at the myriad ways he had drawn the water. The translator's hum changed and she pressed it to her upper-arm where it sent out a snaking tendril, twisting around her arm, gently piercing her skin, linking to her neural network. She opened the journal at the first page.

The water flowed through her cells, plumping out an arm, a leg, swirling through the delicate fronds of her lungs, slithering together the alchemy of her brain and emotions, tasting saliva, moistening membranes and joints, transporting oxygen and nutrients, caressing her muscles, visiting her bones and kidneys, evaporating from her moist skin, in search, again, for other water. The water flowed with her consciousness, floating her eyeballs as she read. It pricked with salty pressure at her eyes.

Jorunn put the book on the ground and wiped at the tears slewing down her cheeks. The grief she felt for Frank and the damaged

Earth planet he wrote about, weighed on her like a great boulder. She looked around at Meanda feeling a new, profound anxiety.

The water was feeling the pull of a moon, moving towards its first high tide. Meanda rotated with its sun and two moons, and the water bulged and retreated in response to their diverse gravities, holding together.

At first light, Jorunn moved down the cliff to the beach, using the horizontal trunks of protruding trees as steps. The cave entrance was concealed behind a dense curtain of waterweed and large, dusty spiderwebs that had achieved the texture of fine wool. She dived into the water, slipped under the curtain and swam along the river into the cave. On the bank she unlooped a rope from its tether and stepped onto her Y-shaped raft. Since midsummer was long gone, there was precious little time to ride out with the ocean tide before it turned and brought her back in again.

Out on the water, she looked back at tangles of gorse and stunt-ed trees on the island, which still clung to the black night, retarding the arrival of dawn. She stood, gently rocking the long, upright, wooden paddle from side to side, but the tide was doing most of the work, carrying her out along the river estuary towards the open sea.

Her paddle worked with the movement of the water, stirring, joining with the water's own eddies and vortices.

She steered along the deeper channel, watching the ghostly yellow shimmer of submerged sandbanks to either side of her. This morning she would not undertake her usual tasks of bringing in fish or searching the mudflats for shellfish and seaweed. The call was her only purpose today.

The tide was near-ready to turn and carry her inland again. Clouds blackened the sky like smoke. She tied off the paddle and slid into the water, swam downwards and opened her mouth to let out the call for a gathering. Her call reverberated, travelling far out into the dark waters.

The water carried the sound, swirling it in ever increasing circles, pushing it through viscous swells, vibrating it against the skulls of myriad swimming Meandans.

Frank moved towards the part of the river where he had seen it. A life-form like that, that built a fish trap, stole his books, must be able to talk, but how could they communicate and what would he say to it? Run! Swim! Get out of here! We're coming to ruin your beautiful planet? There was no trace of her.

A stretch of water offered him glee, invited him in. It pushed him along purposefully. He floated on his back, admiring the blue of the sky, rolled to his front but too late to evade the boulder looming ahead.

A face swam slowly through fog towards him. 'Christ!' Frank tried to sit, to scramble backwards away from it.

'Careful! You've suffered an injury.' Her voice was blurry but he could understand the words.

Frank put a hand to his throbbing head and the leaves bound there. She had rescued him. The contours of her body were wavy, curves everywhere. Was it his shaky consciousness and vision or did she really look like that? She wore a very thin, short dress made from green waterweed. It clung to her breasts but then flared loosely over her bulging stomach. She was … pregnant? Her legs were long; sinuous muscles running up her calves, along her thighs. She had delicate, translucent, webs between her toes and long fingers. She wore a necklace—salt crystals perhaps. Her features were like a mix of human and otter. She smiled at him. Her tiny teeth bent slightly inwards like an eel's.

'You've been unconscious for many days.'

Frank moved slightly, sending a stabbing pain through his head. In response to his perplexed frown as to how they could understand one another, she tapped an armlet with tiny mushrooms sprouting from it, that had wrapped itself around her arm. It shifted occasionally in response to their voices. Some kind of mycelium-based technology. He knew Earth scientists had been working on theories that both water and mycelium had extraterrestrial origins.

He was in a spectacular cave, hearing the slow drips of ages-old, glossy, pink and cream stalactites and stalagmites. Concretions draped from the ceiling like stiff textiles. A few feet from where he lay, a broad river flowed through the cave. Sunlight pierced down from a circular opening far above them.

'Sorry I took your books. They're safe.' She pointed to a neat pile of his gear stacked against the wall. He turned his head to see where she indicated and that's when he caught sight of the drawings.

'My God!' He hauled himself to his feet, using the rocks, first for leverage and then to cling to. His body felt as if it hadn't worked for weeks, but all of that was immaterial besides getting a look at the drawings. Leaning on the uneven wall he staggered towards them. The cave tunnel extended along the underground river, disappearing into darkness. The rock was pale and uneven. Frank marveled at the images of myriad swimmers, depictions of water, fish and birds. Ochre and black drawings swarmed along the wall and around rock outcroppings and disappeared into the blackness beyond the patch of light where Frank and Jorunn stood. 'Did you draw these?'

'Some,' she said, 'and my mother, grandmother, and back, beyond them. Soon,' she smoothed a hand over the round of her stomach, 'my daughter will make her marks of Meanda here too.'

Meanda? Her name for the planet? His own efforts were paltry besides these drawings. His head was spinning and he subsided to the ground, his back to the wall. 'I'm Frank,' he said. 'Thank you for helping me.'

'Jorunn,' she told him. 'I was glad to help you, but your people must not return here, Frank.'

He groaned. He didn't feel up to this conversation. 'We are from another planet, called Earth...'

She gestured impatiently and interrupted him. 'Yes, I know all that. I read your book.' He was astonished to see copious tears sliding down her cheeks. 'I am so sorry, Frank, for your Earth, for your people.'

'Thank you,' he said, bowing his head, feeling an enormous grief … and relief. It seemed like the first time anyone had really, openly mourned for Earth and humanity, the first time he could fully experience that sadness himself. 'I will do what I can to prevent humans from coming here,' he said earnestly.

She looked at him for some time. 'What can you do?'

He wasn't sure. Something. There must be something. He had belonged to a revolutionary group back on Earth that was working on plans to resist the mega-corporations that controlled the governments. He'd grown frustrated and disillusioned with their lack of progress and what felt to him like empty rhetoric. He could rejoin the group, perhaps. Try and give them new impetus from his knowledge of this other life, this other beautiful planet. But would anyone believe him? Would beauty be enough to spur anyone to act? 'I should get back to the ship. They will be looking for me.'

'Yes. They looked for many days.'

'How many days?'

She shrugged. 'Twenty perhaps.'

Frank stared at her. 'But the mission, it was only intended to stay for ten, fifteen tops. The supplies …'

'Yes,' she said. 'They left.'

'Left?'

'Three days ago.'

'The ship left?'

She nodded, absorbed in the task of comprehending his reactions and his facial expressions.

He was stranded here.

'They did search very hard for you,' she said. 'Especially the female with yellow hair.'

'Lena. The captain.'

'Perhaps I should have given you to them, but I thought you were too ill to be moved,' Jorunn said, her face overcome with anxiety.

'No,' he reassured her. 'I was thinking of staying.'

'I read that in your book. *Your* drawings are also beautiful.'

≈

As Frank recovered, he began to accompany Jorunn and learn how she eeked out an existence. She lived by the rhythms of light, tide, moon, seasons. Her thick skin was like an inbuilt wetsuit, keeping her warm. She usually wore a fish-skin bathing suit, moulded to her swelling body. At night she bundled herself up in a garment that looked like otter fur and duck feathers. It covered her from head to foot. She could swim quite well in this too if she needed to. She kept her living waterweed dress tethered in the water, so that it retained its shimmer and tensility. Her body was habituated most to swimming or swaying on her raft. Walking on solid ground, she told him, was to enter a less familiar element.

At first, every time he had to follow Jorunn into a river or the sea, he thought he would die or at least be seriously injured. The seawater slapped boisterously at him from all directions. Sometimes he was sea-sick, swimming with her through its muscular currents. She moved with such assurance and speed, working with the environment, and he was not attuned to that. Gradually, it became easier, until he was feeling the joy of newfound physical capabilities, experiencing a freedom from gravity in the water, galvanised by brine.

The soles of Jorunn's feet and the palms of her hands had suckers, like an octopus, that were tremendously strong, enabling her to run on wet rock and climb up waterfalls. As he learnt more about Meanda and Jorunn he looked with newfound pleasure at the slimy slither of a snail, the inky squirts of a squid and fish spitting sticky threads to reel in prey or fabricate sacs for their eggs. He looked with pleasure at the mottled green mucus slide of an eel and at the crazed salt marshes.

When Jorunn swam she did not slice through the water with her arms, kicking her legs. She bent her body sinuously like a snake, zigzagging with remarkable speed. When she saw how he swam she laughed loudly, gulping great mouthfuls of water and pointing at him. 'Why? Why?'

'It's how I learnt. I don't know how to do it like you.' He tried imitating her movement but was quickly sinking and having to struggle back to the surface. 'My body doesn't bend like yours.'

'But you just have to bend with the water.'

He shook his head. 'I don't know how.'

She pointed at a fish in the river, turning and bending in a silvered flash. 'The fish is swum by the river.'

He watched her run across the marshy ground on the sides of her feet, swift and light. He saw her throw herself blithely into seething waters and disappear into an underground river.

He noticed how the polished caves below ground, with their gnarled landscapes of twisted, thrusting, falling rock and ice, were like a reflection of the cliffs above ground; both formed by the slow, undulating embraces of water and gravity.

There was plenty here to survive on as long as you learnt the ways of the water and the debatable land around it, the places between water and land, the way the water slacked just before the tide began to ebb, and the way it calmed at sunset. Frank knew she was showing him her world in the hope it might enhance the possibility of beneficent human contact, but he knew Meanda would be irreparably damaged by human settlement here.

'Are there more of you?'

'On the other archipelagos.'

'Why do you live alone? Are you outcast?'

'We each live alone. One to each archipelago. We like it that way. We meet briefly to mate.'

'There are very few of you, then.'

'There are enough.'

'You are like the nymph of this archipelago.' She shrugged, not understanding him. 'How did you choose a mate?'

'It seemed a good time. I was at a gathering.'

Frank swallowed down a stab of jealousy. 'Aren't you lonely?' he asked her.

'No!' Her laugh burst from her gleefully. 'I'm surrounded with companions!'

Frank's gaze followed her gesturing hand. 'Companions?'

'Fish, birds, trees, and the water of course, and soon Isla will come, my child, and I will teach her.'

She took him to the top of the cliff to look out across her archipelago and down on the rivers and streams twisting across the islands. 'The little river tributaries number more than your eyelashes,' he told her.

She smiled, but then her face turned serious. 'Other Meandans will come soon, to discuss your expedition, in response to the call I sent.'

The water moved them, massed them in the surf as they headed for Jorunn's island. It slid and swirled around the curves of their shoulders, hips and ankles.

Frank and Jorunn waited on the beach at dawn, listening to the clattering drag of pebbles, trying to see through the sea fret. At first, Frank distinguished a few dark heads in the water, bobbing closer and closer. 'I see eight!' he called excitedly to Jorunn, as if he were a child spotting seals. She stood a few metres away on the shell-scattered beach. She frowned. Frank edged towards her. 'Am I in danger?'

Her glance was compassionate. 'Perhaps … yes.'

The first rank of Meandans reached the shallow water and began to wade. Some held children by the hand and others had babies perched on their shoulders, clinging to their long hair. Behind these first few, Frank saw hundreds more heads in the water, hundreds more shoulders cresting the surface. He had never been afraid of Jorunn, but now he felt fear at the sheer number of those who were other than him.

Some of those walking up the beach towards Frank had patches of crusted salt on their shoulders and cheeks, or their skin was streaked with bright green waterweed. One male approached Jorunn laughing, showing her the livid pink welt of a severe jellyfish sting on his chest. They massed on the beach like a great, dark rookery of seals, and there were around a thousand of them in all.

Frank backed away. 'Is this all of you?' he whispered to Jorunn, finding that he was now standing right next to her.

'No. Only those within a ten-day swim.'

The gathering went on for three days. Frank and the human encroachment were the main item for discussion but they saved that for last, so that he gained a view of their society in action in relation to other, smaller matters, first. Their population was stable because of their unsocial living patterns. All species lived in mutual harmony and balance, in equality and autonomy.

All life was seen to have value, to be tied together in dynamic networks of mutual interdependence. If there was a conflict between the rights of one life-form and another, then the Meandans held a dilemma resolution council. It didn't happen often. It was not in an archipelago occupant's interest to damage their own habitat. In general, they gave priority to the needs of other species, before their own. There were people with specialised knowledge who acted as advocates for other voiceless life-forms: fish advocates, tree advocates, mycelium advocates, and Jorunn, it transpired, was a water advocate. 'It's the oldest life-form on the planet,' she told Frank, 'but it's extraterrestrial, like the mycelium, like you. The water travelled here from a spring in space. I will remind them of this. It may tell in your favour.'

On Jorunn's island a rogue beast, that looked like a dog-size rhinoceros, had been killing other beasts, many more than it needed for sustenance. After an advocate had spoken for the rhinoceros, they decided it was in the best interest to capture and relocate it. Two hunters stood, armed with spears, and ran in the direction Jorunn indicated. Frank swallowed. Is that what might happen to him? Herded into exile at the end of those sharpened-bone spears? But where could they put him?

Finally, they came to Jorunn's report on the human expedition. She introduced Frank and he explained the situation on Earth, warning that the settlers were likely to return. It was unnecessary to tell them of the threat. They understood it clearly enough from his description of the degradation of Earth's environment. A special advocates council was convened, including one to represent all the Meandans. Jorunn told him this had never happened before: a council for the whole planet. They went into the water for their deliberations. 'Why into the water?' Frank asked bemused, as she prepared to walk down to the water's edge with the others.

'Because the water will help us make the right decision.'

He watched anxiously as the ten Meandans moved into the sea. They were out there for hours. Frank grew tired of watching and waiting and struck up a conversation with one of the males. At first he gestured to Frank to be patient while his mycelium translator wrapped around his arm plugging itself into his neural network;

then they talked about Frank's drawings and the pictures in the caves.

'They're coming out now,' the male said, nodding towards the shore.

The ten advocates emerged, with Jorunn smiling broadly and a tiny baby perched on her shoulder, gripping her hair. 'You...?' Frank began, as she passed the child to him.

'Yes.' She said. 'Here is Isla.' A huge pair of turquoise eyes regarded Frank earnestly.

The advocates had decided to negotiate if the humans returned. If the explorers would not comply with the balance they would be resisted. Frank kept his doubt about the Meandans' capacity to resist to himself. One male stood and pointed at Frank. 'What about him? He does not belong here. He disturbs the balance.'

All faces turned towards Frank. He swallowed. Isla was still in his arms. He looked at Jorunn. She stood and spoke for him. 'Look at his drawings of Meanda.' She passed around the drawings. Those at the front of the crowd held them between themselves and their neighbours, exclaiming quietly. 'He does not upset the balance,' Jorunn asserted. 'Meanda and the water are happy to absorb him.'

There was a long silence. The drawings were being passed back through the crowd and those in the front rank were smiling. 'They allow you,' Jorunn whispered.

The Meandans returned to the sea and their archipelagos. Frank expected to live with Jorunn and her daughter, but instead, she established him on his own island and told him they would visit once in a while. 'This way,' she said, 'you will learn to survive and live in balance.' He was the occupant of his own island, but it was a lonely existence in between their visits.

The water flowed upwards towards the sky as sap inside a great willow, cascading as a silvery waterfall of rustling, draping leaves.

Isla and Frank stood on the riverbank. She had grown as tall as his waist and easily outstripped him in learning how to live with their environment. Patiently, she tried again to teach him how to spot the really tasty fish. They flinched at a heavy boom in the sky, louder than any thunder. Frank knew what he was looking at. 'Quick, get in the water, Isla! Swim and tell Jorunn the humans have returned.' She moved towards the bank.

But it was too late. Lena and four crew members stood before them. Frank experienced a rapid flush of emotions at the sight of them. He was relieved to see them, his own, familiar kind, especially Lena. But what did their appearance mean for his idyll here? What did it mean for Jorunn and Isla, for Meanda?

'Frank! Still alive I see,' Lena said. He moved to put a protective arm around the child. 'And right, too, about the life-forms here.' Lena was staring, wide-eyed, at the details of Isla's difference. Two crewmen stepped towards them. 'We need to take it back to the ship to study it,' Lena said.

'She's not a specimen,' Frank said angrily.

'Is she yours?'

'Yes,' he lied.

Lena tched. 'They won't like that. Murdon and the other sponsors won't like that.'

'I don't give a fuck what Murdon will or won't like.' Isla's great turquoise eyes looked up at him in alarm, hearing the anger in his voice. She clung to him like seaweed.

'No choice about that Frank,' Lena said.

'Lena,' Frank made a desperate attempt. 'They are intelligent. More intelligent than us I would say. The planet is seething with them,' he lied. 'It's no good for Murdon.'

'Seething?' she frowned. 'We're still not showing anything on the instrumentation. Except we found your body-heat signature and so landed this little fish.' She looked with something like friendliness at Isla.

'She's not a fish. She is a Meandan; intelligent semi-aquatic.' Frank didn't want to tell her the instrumentation wasn't showing them because of the depths of the caves and oceans. 'Our rule is, if there is intelligent indigenous life on a planet, we leave that planet alone.'

'Those *were* the rules, Frank,' she sighed, 'but things have gotten a whole lot worse. We are in the endgame now, on Earth. Our orders are to make this planet habitable for Murdon's settlement fast, no matter what. They'll be here within weeks. They don't have any other options left.'

The thought of the rapacious, selfish Wealths trampling here horrified him but he had to play for time to help the Meandans to respond. 'Then let me negotiate with the Meandans. Explain the situation.'

Lena looked at him sadly. 'We have to test her, Frank, you know that.'

He could guess at her orders. Study the life-forms and then exterminate them, whether or not they posed any threat, because they would be competing for resources. The experience of Earth had taught The Wealths that sharing was not a preferred option. 'I won't let them hurt you,' he assured Isla, holding her gaze to reassure her. Then he looked at Lena and the crew members: two men and two women. Could he take them? Their five against his one? His time on Meanda had honed his muscles but they were all in good shape too. Nevertheless, he watched for the best moment to launch an attack. He just needed enough time to allow Isla to escape. 'Let us go, Lena. Find somewhere else.'

'I can't do that.' She looked with sad tenderness at Isla. 'Perhaps the sponsors won't want to come to this exoplanet with *you* on it, Frank, especially if you're breeding with some fish.'

Frank ignored the jibe and the hint of jealousy in her tone.

'The Wealths regard *us* as another species, Frank. An unwanted one. They will consider *you* a toxic factor here.' Lena grimaced.

'Let us go, Lena. You know you don't believe in what you're doing. Why should we, any of us,' he addressed all of them, 'do the bidding of The Wealths now. Aren't all bets off? Nothing from our old lives matters. Surely, nothing, except that we do the right thing, act right?'

Lena's expression shifted from hesitation, back to resolve. Her communicator rang, and Frank saw Murdon's jowled face appear onscreen. The signal was bad. 'Uprising …' The link dropped. Lena and the team were distracted as they fiddled anxiously with their technology.

Frank edged Isla further away from them and nearer to the river bank. 'Go!' The water received her rapid entry with a soft sigh of relief, instead of a splash.

Lena and the crew looked up. 'Frank!' Lena stared at him.

The two crewmen ran to the river, their weapons drawn, but Frank knew Isla was long gone. They had no hope of catching her. Thwarted, they gripped Frank's arms and pinioned them behind him. They pulled him to stand alongside Lena. He looked at the snow blizzard of empty pixels on her screen; listened to its white noise. Suddenly, the device resuscitated. The face on the screen was not Murdon's. 'Captain, you must return to Earth.'

'Where's Murdon?'

'Dead. Overthrown by the revolution. Get back here, Captain.' The crew members gasped.

'Will do.' She closed the connection. The crewmen let go of Frank. Struggling with him was suddenly pointless. Lena and the crew exchanged shocked glances. 'There has been increasing resistance but this is amazing....' Lena's expression was undecided between delight and fear.

She moved apart from the others with Frank. 'I'll wipe Meanda from the star charts,' she said in a low voice. 'Good luck Frank.'

He took her hand. 'You could stay, Lena. You and the crew. Your chances will be better here. The Meandans will accept a small number of you. Humans don't have a good track record with revolution any more than with ecology.'

Lena nodded, smiled regretfully. 'Bye, Frank.'

Jorunn stood waiting for him, clasping Isla to her hip.

'Frank saved me,' Isla told her mother.

'Are the humans coming?' Jorunn asked. 'I sent the call but the others will not be here for a few days. We should shelter in the caves until then.'

'It's alright. The humans aren't coming.'

Frank told her about the revolution and Lena's erasure of the Meanda expedition records. Relief blossomed on Jorunn's face. They turned together towards the cave but then Frank stopped.

'What is it, Frank?'

'I should return to Earth.'

Jorunn stared at him.

'Perhaps I can help now. Take back the knowledge you and Meanda have given me. I know Earth will not return to a paradise in my lifetime, but we can help the water to start the process.'

She nodded. 'The water wants that, Frank.'

Slowly he looked around him, taking in the view, then Jorunn and Isla's faces, like a last lungful of air against drowning. His eyes clouded with bitter water. He looked up at the Earth ship still in orbit and hoped that Lena would wait for him this time.

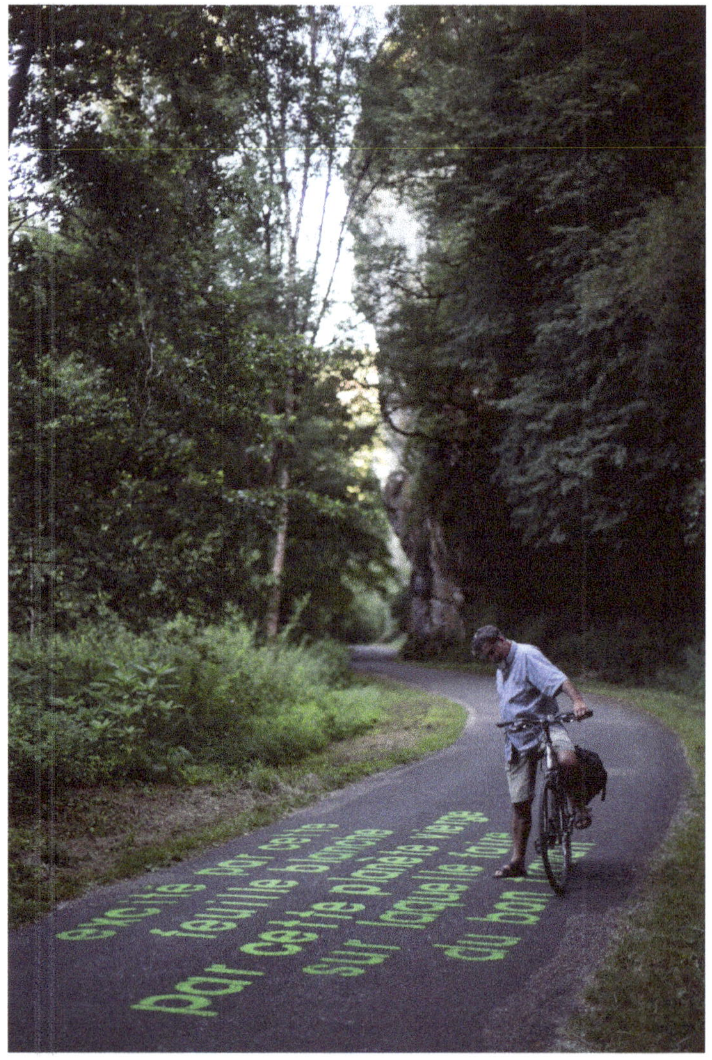

Tracey Warr, *Meanda*, 2016. Installed text on the GR36 path beside the River Lot near Saint Cirq Lapopie, France, in the *Exoplanet Lot* exhibition organised by Maison des Arts Georges et Claude Pompidou. Photo by Yohann Gozard.

The Extraterrestrial

water
springing in the milky way
travelling through space
incising cliffs and caves
in slow undulating embraces with
gravity
glossing stalactites and stalagmites
puddling condensing humid and damp
mist braiding around itself
residing in clouds for nine days
falling as rain and dew
hungry and leaching minerals
playing with light and oxygen
rolling back and forth with the moon

turbulent in vortices eddies and spates
calming reveries
melting
stroking purple waterlilies
navigating archipelagos
splashed by coypus
resonating creaking frogs
meandering sluggish with dissolved material
blooming viscous ice
and bludgeoning shards of hail
geysering high
thundering in glassy sheets
hanging in fat droplets reflecting the world
sitting in tiny balls cohering
blue green brown silvery with moonlight and dawn
streaked with flashes of turquoise bioluminescence
gyring and gimbling
ripples riffles glides and deep liquid pockets
glitter paths of tiny reflected suns
tangling tresses of aquatic plants
beneath inscrutable surfaces
exquisite complexities of liquid light and reflections
slick sleek sinuous
moving towards high tide
slapping boisterously in muscular currents
galvanised by brine
slacking just before ebb tide calming at sunset

clattering pebbles below sea frets

crazing and crusting salt marshes

flowing through cells plumping skin

swirling in the delicate fronds of lungs

slithering together the alchemy of thought and emotion

tasting saliva

moistening membranes

caressing muscles

flowing with consciousness

floating eyeballs pricking with the salty pressure of tears

slimy slithers of snails

inky squirts of squid and fish spitting sticky threads

mottled green mucus slide of eels

fish turning and bending in silvered flashes

flowing upwards towards the sky as sap inside a willow

sloshing deep in the mantle

leaking through cracks in ocean beds

as serpentine and olivine rocks

spewing from volcanic vents

in search again for other

FORD

humit

wet

rosada

dew

toll

puddle

els petits afluents del riu són més nombrosos que les teves pesta-
nyes

the little tributaries of the river are more in number than your
eyelashes

som analfabets de l'aigua?

are we water illiterate?

gual, on els humans troben aigua

ford, where human meets water

riera

brook

rierol

stream

l'aigua té 4,4 bilions d'anys d'antiguetat, un viatger de l'espai des de
la Via Làctia

water is 4.4 billion years old, a space traveller from the Milky Way

l'aigua que bevem ha estat a la bufeta d'un Tiranosaure rex i a molts
altres llocs

the water you drink has been through the bladder of a Tyrannosau-
rus rex and many other places

font

spring

torrent

torrent

abeurador

watering hole

corrent

flowing

cascada

falling

saltiró

tumbling

xipolleig

splashing

bombolles

bubbling

meandre

meander

remolí

eddy

vòrtex

vortex

oxigen i hidrogen s'aparellen

oxygen and hydrogen mating

la matriu de tota la vida

the matrix of all life

el detergent mata la motilitat de l'aigua

detergent kills the motility of water

metamorfosi com a vapor, boira, núvols, pluja, aiguaneu, neu, ca-
lamarsa, gel

metamorphoses as vapour, mist, cloud, rain, sleet, snow, hail, ice

l'aigua passa nou dies al cel i torna a caure

water spends nine days in the sky and falls again

les diferents olors d'aigua: després de la pluja, en una tomaquera, la
olor de la neu, de la humitat

the different smells of water: after rain, on a tomato plant, the smell
of snow, of humidity

simplement separant l'herba com la clenxa als cabells en el seu ori-
gen, brollant amb turbulents confluències, clapotejant a través de
maresmes salades fins a la desemboca

merely parting the grass at its source, like a parting in your hair,
gushing through turbulent confluences, squelching across salt
marshes to its estuary

erosions lentes, modelant la terra

slow erosions, shaping the land

el menisc d'una gota d'aigua

the meniscus of a water drop

boira creixent al riu de matinada

mist rising off the morning river

arrauxada

lulling

hipnòtica

hypnotic

en cascada

cascading

atronadora

thundering

viscositat de l'aigua, aferrament de les molècules d'aigua entre elles, encolant el món

stickiness of water, clinginess of water molecules for each other, gluing the world

conques

watersheds

aqüífers

aquifers

aigües subterrànies

underground waters

roques hidratades anomenades serpentina profunda en el mantell de la Terra

hydrous rocks called serpentine deep in the Earth's mantle

redistribucions dramàtiques de l'aigua del planeta

dramatic redistributions of the planet's water

les desigualtats amb l'aigua

water inequalities

els conflictes per l'aigua

water conflicts

les migracions per l'aigua

water migrations

allunyar-se de les aigües

retreating from the waters

rius eren les antigues carreteres principals

rivers were the old main roads

els nostres cossos i els nostres entorns han estat dissenyats per l'aigua

our bodies and our environments are engineered by water

una de cada 2.500 persones tenen els dits dels peus o de les mans
palmejats—sindactília

1 in 2,500 people have webbed toes or fingers—syndactyly

la verda tranquillitat d'estar sobre i dins del riu

the green tranquillity of being on and in the river

somiant amb anar a una altra banda

dreaming of going elsewhere

descobriments submergits: eureka!

immersed discoveries: eureka!

el corrent de la consciència sense bretxa, crac o divisió

the stream of consciousness without breach, crack or division

la joia del riu a l'estiu

the glee of the summer river

l'amenaça de la veloç aigua tèrbola en crescuda, carregada de runa

the threat of the fast brown water in spate, loaded with debris

la inundació corrent carrers avall, inundant jardins, inventant nous llacs de cignes i camallargs

the flooding river running down streets, swamping gardens, inventing new lakes for swans and waders

gongoozling = veient la vida passar pel riu

gongoozling = watching life go by on the river

l'esgarip plaent de llançar-se un mateix al riu

the delighted yelp of throwing yourself in the river

anar amb la corrent

go with the flow

aigua dolça, aigua salobre, aigua salada, llàgrimes salades, llavis de sal

freshwater, brackish water, saltwater, salt tears, salt lips

rentat i no escrit per l'aigua

washed and unwritten by water

The Water Age

She was getting on my nerves. In my face. In my space. I could feel the ink rising in me like bile. Like Tourette's.

'Urgh!' She screamed, her voice drowning, gargling ink.

Her face was covered in bright blue ink. It drooled from her lower lip and her clumped eyelashes as she blinked at me in disbelief.

It dripped globules from her fringe. Snaked down her neck. Stained the collar of her pale shirt.

'Urgh! You ...' She couldn't find speech for it. She shook her hands where ink dripped now too, after she had swiped them across her eyes.

I raised my eyebrows appreciatively. The squid graft had taken better than expected. But, drat. I hadn't even managed to hone the ink into a well-crafted sentence of rebuke. Not even a word. I'd just spat and spluttered it at her. Thank goodness it wasn't toxic. I hadn't gone that far with my hybridising experiments on myself. It wouldn't do to be murdering people because they irritated me. I was astonished it had worked so well but concerned to think about how I could go forward to combine the ink squirting with my emotional chemistry. I tried to guestimate the amount of the ink squirt by looking at her, but she was confusing things now by mixing tears with the ink. There'd be snot and saliva to calibrate in soon. She turned and ran from me silently. The territory was mine.

Asbrú

[Surmised to be an extract from a postgraduate student's transcribed recordings dating from November 2005. The author is unidentified and cannot be located.]

To Whom It May Concern,

The Base is bleak at the turn of the season towards winter with horizontal rain and banshee winds whistling through the old heating pipes and stirring the curtains despite the window seals.

Gaining clear information on the algae research being carried out in the Symbiosis Lab is proving extremely difficult. There appear to be four research sections: Modifications, Temporalities, Communications and Statistical Analysis. I have been informed that the personnel numbers twelve scientists—three in each section—a total of eight men and four women. However, when I arrived to carry out my interviews only three scientists were present: two in the Modifications Section and one in the Communications Section. I have not succeeded in making contact with the others. The project start date was 1971.

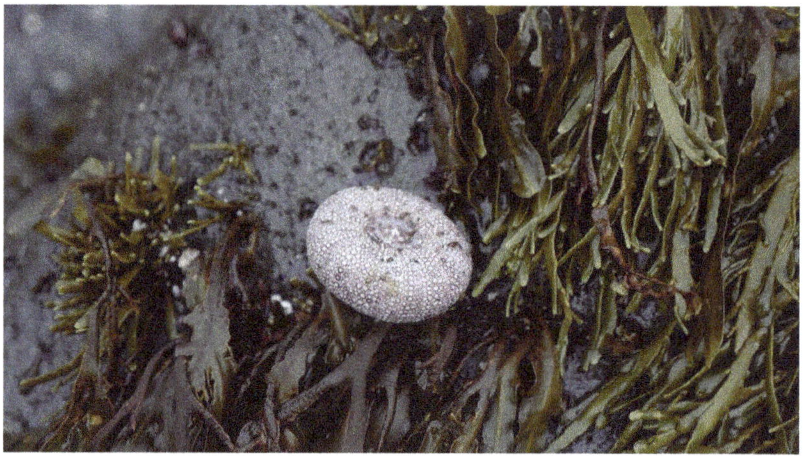

Urchin and algae, Iceland. Jutempus, *Zooetics Future Fictions Summit*, 2017. Part of *Frontiers in Retreat*. Photo by Nomeda Urbonas.

I carried out a series of interviews with one of the researchers, but many of my questions went unanswered. Did soldiers volunteer for the project? Were there casualties? Have any casualties been identified? It seems that some scientists, soldiers and an artist are missing, or at least not available for interview. I have been unable to ascertain what happened to them.

I asked: What was the aim of this symbiosis project? To produce a superhuman, an aquahuman? My interview subject responded: No. The aim is to establish interspecies communication and awareness, to share knowledge, to address future environmental imbalance.

'To share knowledge with the algae?' I asked, unable to keep the incredulity from my voice. I received no response.

It appears that the research team eventually started experimenting on themselves, and all of the researchers in the Temporalities and Statistical Analysis Sections were involved in that. I wondered how they managed to record their results as they entered increasingly algae-like states. They seem to have decided that they had to try to bring back subjective information. The observations they have been recording appear to be reducing, at least in any recognisable form.

How long do you think the symbiosis took to take effect? I mean, this is a system that is still working, right? I asked the researcher. Have you gotten in the tanks yourself? What effect will The Base closure have on this research? How are you planning to conclude and disseminate your results? The researcher pulled a face and shrugged. The meaning of the response was not clear.

There are vibrations coming down the swim pipe to the tidal tanks, song maybe. The only way to find out more appears to be a physical encounter of my own. [The writer's account breaks off here.]

Extracts from the Red Book Research Reports

[This Red Book was found in the deserted lab. Dates have been obscured by water damage.]

Research Section 1: Modifications

Working Hypothesis—symbiosis, new indication capacities, interspecies communication and knowledge enabling counteraction of predicted progress towards hypertrophy and entropy. Without radically new knowledge enabling shifts in culture and actions, our futurecasts and all projections display rapid trajectory through health damage, environmental damage, hypertrophy of exploitation, hypertrophy of the environment, hypertrophy of humanity and ecological disbalance.

In Stage 1, subjects began a programme of algae ingestions, soaking in tidal algae tanks, eel windings. Initial tidal immersions were undertaken with breathing apparatus and tethers. After one week bacteria patches were applied. Varying individual tolerances to high levels of iodine noted. Psychosomatic/placebo effects factored in. Obs. after one month included increased body fat and hair; significantly increased mucilage. Second month: applications of sea snails, slugs, crabs, urchins. Continued immersions and ingestions.

Obs: Enhanced taste capacities particularly in savoury, salty range; vastly enhanced salt tolerance; pigmentation shifts (greening of hair and skin); thickening of skin which is demonstrating patches of heavily whorled textures. Series of losses of volunteers and conscripts has necessitated some self-experimentation to maintain the research schedule.

In Stage 2, feet developed holdfast complexes. Under-skin vesicles (grape-like air bubbles) developed, particularly clustered around collar-bone area. Arms have lengthened and are tending towards frond-like flagellata. Experiencing increased difficulty in releasing holdfasts. Obs.: regulating body temperature for cold water; osmoregulation; development of conceptacle cavities containing viable reproductive organs. Rhythmic shifts in verticality and horizontality observed i.e., subjects are erect during sea immersions and layered horizontally in periods of air exposure.

In Stage 3, subjects are demonstrating increased blindness and reliance on enhanced haptic, tactile and olfactory capabilities. Tethers are no longer necessary since holdfasts are functioning adequately for anchorage. Flattening and softening of skeletal structure and tendency to apical morphology noted. Extreme alterations in the body's bearing structure to cope with water pressures and non-motility are developing. Increased mucilage from genitals, nose, mouth, ears, eyes evident, and enabling repeated, prolonged immersions. Vesicles are making underwater breathing feasible for duration of tidal immersions. Subjects appear to be integrating with surrounding algae community and are displaying mixotrophic energy derivation.

Research Section 2: Temporalities

Taking into consideration that green algae are thought to be in the evolutionary line that gave rise to the first land plants, the conducted experiments attempted to investigate a constant encounter between humans and algae, as a newly installed and technologically tested symbiotic interaction. Although the optimum methodology has not yet been determined, the consumption of different species of seaweeds, inhalation of the algae extracts, algae skin applications, and reproduction of aquatic environment of algae had an effect on the circadian, biological and social rhythms of the participants, producing the effect of desynchronisation and resynchronisation along the axis of what is traditionally called a human temporal structure.

Depending on species and quantities used, and varying according to individual tolerances to high levels of iodine (in particular, its effect on thyroid functioning), amount of light and water, different algaematic sets caused accelerations and slow-downs within the system of metabolism, blood circulation, functioning of hormone system, processes of rejuvenation and senescence as well as increase or decrease in exposure to extreme temperatures, mental activity, attention span, memory storage capacity, enhancement or diminishment of sensations, improvement or weakening of IQ, boost or decline in activity of imagination etc.

Participants report that the algae experiments are having a 'dehumanising impact on the perception of time'. One subject was unable to report his experience of time shift in words but, instead, drew spherical curves representing rhythmical shifts of human-algae symbiotic interaction. Human perception of time appears to be intertwining with different temporalities imposed by marine plants and we, consequently, propose a speculative notion of 'aquatic time'.

Research Section 3: Communications

Attempting cross-species translation of perception and cross-species learning to counteract projected ecological disbalance. Analysis of communication arising from symbiosis to assist in developing a programme for biosphere equilibrium. Initially, other modalities appear incomprehensible. Symbiosis may produce results leading to enhanced understanding of the optimum operations at all levels: atmosphere, lithosphere, pedosphere, biosphere, hydrosphere, cosmosphere.

Early obs.: initial immersions producing sleep-like, trance-like consciousness shifts; the mouth can function as a knowledge sensor; ingesting, digesting, metabolic structure, playing a role in consciousness. Nothing intelligible yet, however, embodied sensory dialogue with algae appears increasingly likely.

Subjects are reading wave power, wind strength and direction, tides, phases of the moon. Subjects are able to taste impacts from chemical and other marine contaminants. We have been able to derive what appear to be algae sensing and desires; plans even.

Analysis of sounds and vibrations created by the kelp colonisation of the severed acoustic sea-cables is in progress.

No tangible results from artist's residency. Artist is missing, possibly as a consequence of inappropriate algae contact.

Struggling now to keep communication channels open as symbiosis progresses further.

Research Section 4: Statistical Analysis

Analysis of algology symbiosis evidences positive results. Some subjects demonstrate adaptation to tidal and seasonal rhythms. Greatly enhanced consciousness of interscalar and trans-systemic relationships are being recorded. Prolonged rhythmic immersions are resulting in reflexive consciousness, a form of self-archaeology.

Consequent to this aquatic marine research phase, further symbiotic exploration is planned involving freshwater, aerial, lichenic, parasitic and motile algae.

Planning timescale needs to change to 100 years or more.

Visions of new ecologies glimpsed.

Confronting light is the darkness.

The awe-ful rainbow.

[Reports break off.]

Notes

p. 1   'Earth's Lament' is based on a 13th century love lament by the female troubadour, Comtesse de Dia (see Bogin, Meg (1980) *The Women Troubadours*, New York: W.W. Norton). I wrote the song for the *Exoplanet Lot* exhibition as part of a collaborative performance with artist, Tania Candiani. The lament was sung in Occitan. The recording was played at the bottom of the Lot Valley cliff at Saint Cirq Lapopie and listened to through Tania Candiani's *Landscape Sound Amplifier* sculpture. *Exoplanet Lot* was co-curated by Martine Michard, Rob La Frenais and Ludwig and organised by Maison des Arts Georges et Claude Pompidou, Cajarc in July-September 2016.

p. 5   An earlier version of 'Meanda' was written in residence at Maison Daura in Saint Cirq Lapopie, France and published in English and French as an e-book for the *Exoplanet Lot* exhibition organised by Maison des Arts Georges et Claude Pompidou, Cajarc in July 2016. A version of 'Meanda' was also published as twitter fiction on @Meanda55555 in 2016. Extracts from the French text were temporarily installed along the GR36 Route (to Compostella) where it runs beside the River Lot near Saint Cirq Lapopie and at La Source Zen café on the River Lot, where a 'Meanda Reading Room' with waterlily pond and books attached to buoys were also installed.

p. 37　'The Extraterrestrial' was a circular text installed on the ground in chalk around the 19th century Armstrong Hydraulic Engine in Allenheads village, Northumberland, UK, in June 2016 as part of the *As Above So Below* project organised by Allenheads Contemporary Arts. The engine hisses perpetually with the sound and power of suppressed water.

p. 41　'FORD' was developed during a residency I undertook at Centre d'Art i Natura in Farrera in the Catalan Pyrenees in 2015 as part of *Frontiers in Retreat*. 'FORD' was presented as an ephemeral intervention in Catalan and English at the ford where the Barranc de Farrera stream crosses the footpath near Farrera in the *SAÓ Festival—Art and Nature in the High Pyrenees* on 11 October 2015. Apologies for any errors in the Catalan. The translation was achieved through a mixture of Google Translate and friendly help. 'FORD' is documented on www.farreracan.cat/sao and included in the online exhibition, *Edge Effects,* www.frontiersinretreat.org/edge-effects/exhibitions/centre_d_art_i_natura_can.

The sources I drew on for the texts were:

Alexandersson, Olof (1990) *Living Water: Viktor Schauberger and the Secrets of Natural Energy*, Dublin: Gateway.

Cheever, John (1990) 'The Swimmer' in *Collected Stories*, London: Vintage.

Deakin, Roger (2000) *Waterlog: A Swimmer's Journey Through Britain*, London: Vintage.

Fishman, Charles (2011) *The Big Thirst: The Secret Life and Turbulent Future of Water*, New York: Free Press.

Franks, Felix (1984) *Water*, London: Royal Society of Chemistry.

James, William (2000) *The Principles of Psychology*, vol. 1, London: Dover.

Joyce, James (1939) *Finnegans Wake*, London: Faber & Faber.

Keats, John, Letter to John Hamilton Reynolds, Oxford, 21 September 1817 keats-poems.com/to-john-hamilton-reynolds-oxford-september-21th-1817/.

Wilkens, Andreas; Jacobi, Michael & Schwenk, Wolfram (2002) *Understanding Water: Developments from the Work of Theodor Schwenk*, Edinburgh: Floris.

and see my collaboration with Urbonas Studio at Modern Art Oxford www.vilma.cc/river.

p. 53   'The Water Age' was written in residency at HIAP—Helsinki International Artist Programme, on Suomenlinna Island, Finland and drew on research on aquatic life and slime technologies that I carried out while in Finland and also during a residency with Urbonas Studio in Cambridge, Massachusetts.

p. 55   'Asbrú' was written on the Asbrú former US air and navy base in Iceland during the *Zooetics Future Fiction Summit* in 2016, which was a collaborative project by Nomeda and Gediminas Urbonas, Tinna Grétarsdottir and Sigurjón Baldur Hafsteinsson, Oksana Anilionyte, Nikola Bojic, Gardar Eyjólfsson, Lucas Freeman, Ashley Rizzo Moss, Thomas Pausz, Kristupas Sabolius, Viktorija Siaulyte, Hildigunnur Sverrisdóttir, Sigrun Thorlacius and myself. A version of the text was presented in performance by Gediminas Urbonas at Reykjavik Art Museum on 22 October 2016.

Thanks

I first dreamt up the notion of The Water Age during the *Learning from the River* week-long workshop that I ran at MIT with Gediminas Urbonas in 2012. My thanks to the participants in that first workshop, especially Gediminas, Nomeda Urbonas and Giacomo Castagnola. I am also especially grateful to Kurt Hasselbach, the curator of the Hart Nautical Collections at MIT Museum in Cambridge, Massachusetts, who first made me see how a fish is swum by the river and who memorably remarked that we cannot be expected to care about the environment if we cannot get in it.

With regard to The Water Age books themselves, I am very grateful to HIAP and the *Frontiers in Retreat* project for financial support to produce the books. I am also indebted to the staff at HIAP, especially Jenni Nurmenniemi, Jaana Eskola and Salla

Lahtinen for the humane support they extended to me! I am immensely grateful to James A. Hudson for his work on the book covers. And thank you to the photographers and artists who gave me permission to reproduce the images included in this book.

The fictions in this book were developed as part of my work in the *Frontiers in Retreat* project. From 2014–2018 I was an invited artist in this five-year art and ecology research project, which was led by HIAP—Helsinki International Artist Programme. There were 25 invited artists in the project and eight curatorial partners in Finland, Iceland, Latvia, Lithuania, Scotland, Serbia and Catalonia/Spain. The project is documented at www.frontiersinretreat.org and in two publications: *Frontiers in Retreat*, edited by Salla Lahtinen and Jenni Nurmenniemi (HIAP, 2017) and *The Midden*, edited by Jenni Nurmenniemi and Tracey Warr (Garret, 2018). My work in *Frontiers in Retreat* involved visits to several islands: Suomenlinna, Harakka and Utö in Finland and to Iceland. I was in residence on Suomenlinna with HIAP for a total of three months during 2015–2017. These residencies were highly influential for the writing of these texts. Thanks to Tuula Närhinen for the inspiring visit to her studio on Harakka Island.

I worked with Jutempus to develop the *Zooetics* project in *Frontiers in Retreat*, which playfully and poetically explored more-than-human epistemologies. This project was a tremendous inspiration for the writings in this book. I would like to express my gratitude to Jutempus (Nomeda and Gediminas Urbonas) and to Viktorija Siaulyte. Also to Dionizas Litvaitis who did so much to generate a buzz of excitement around the *Zooetics* project in its initial stages. And thanks to all the inspiring contributors to the *Zooetics* Lecture Series, which you can find on YouTube and Vimeo, and to the participants in the *Zooetics Future Fiction Summit* (zooetics.net).

Many of the ideas for The Water Age series were inspired by the triple river estuary at Carmarthen Bay, which I commuted across once a week by train for several years when I lived in Pembrokeshire, Wales. I undertook research on flood predictions in relation to climate change. Work on developing my writing was enabled at an early stage by a Literature Wales Writer's Bursary supported by The National Lottery through the Arts Council of Wales.

Periods spent living in the valleys of the River Lot and the River Viaur in France were also important for the development of these texts.

Many other fiction and non-fiction writers impacted on my ideas about water, especially Tristan Gooley, Roger Deakin, J.G. Ballard, Ursula Le Guin, Doris Lessing and Stanislaw Lem.

The *Exoplanet Lot* residency and exhibition was an exhilarating experience. Thanks to the co-curators: Martine Michard, Rob La Frenais and Ludwig and to my fellow artists in residence: Tania Candiani, HeHe, Thomas Lasbouygues, Caroline Le Méhaute and

Ludwig. And a special thank you to La Source Zen café and Carlos and Christine Hopps for their help with the Meanda waterlily reading room.

Thanks to Helen Ratcliffe and Alan Smith at Allenheads Contemporary Arts for inviting me to participate in *As Above So Below*, 2016.

I was in residence at Centre d'Art i Natura in Farrera in the Catalan Pyrenees for a total of two months during 2015–2016 as part of *Frontiers in Retreat*. I am immensely grateful to Lluís Llobet, Cesca Gelabert and Arnau Llobet for their knowledge, conversation and kindness.

And finally, thanks to Ronald Javier Martin at MIT for his tips on slime technologies research. I hope to do more with those tips in future fiction to come.

ABOUT THE AUTHOR

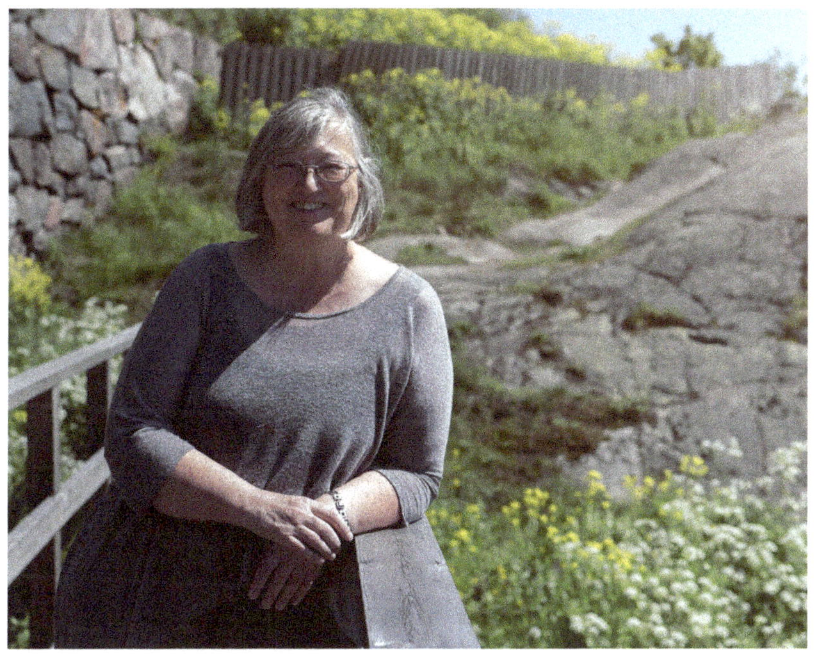

Tracey Warr. Photo by Sergio Urbina.

Tracey Warr is a fiction and non-fiction writer based in France. She describes herself as writing in the vicinity of art. She is an avid swimmer.

Tracey Warr's historical novels, set in France, England and Wales, are published by Meanda Books: *Almodis the Peaceweaver* (2011), *The Viking Hostage* (2014), *Conquest I: Daughter of the Last King* (2016), *Conquest II: The Drowned Court* (2017) and *Conquest III: The Anarchy* (2020). Her fiction has received awards from Literature Wales and Santander and was shortlisted for the Impress Prize.

Her published work on contemporary art includes *The Artist's Body* (Phaidon, 2000), *Remote Performances in Nature and Architecture* (Routledge, 2015) and *The Midden* (Garret, 2018). She has published numerous essays on contemporary artists with publishers including Intellect, Tate, Merrell/Barbican, Black Dog and Manchester University Press. She was an invited artist in the *Exoplanet Lot* exhibition and the *Frontiers in Retreat* five-year art and ecology research project.

She is working on a biography entitled *Three Female Lords,* about three sisters who lived in southern France and northern Spain in the 11th century. The biography has been supported by an Authors' Foundation Award.

She was Head of Dartington Arts School and established MA Poetics of Imagination there with Martin Shaw. She was Programme Lead in art history and theory at Oxford Brookes University and at Dartington College of Arts in the UK. She was Guest Professor at Bauhaus University, Weimar, Germany; MIT,

Cambridge, US; and Piet Zwart Institute, Rotterdam, Netherlands. She was Course Leader in Art History at Saint Francis University Study Abroad Programme in France. She has led many creative writing and art writing courses and workshops.

https://meandabooks.com
https://traceywarrwriting.com
www.facebook.com/traceywarrARTwriting
www.facebook.com/traceywarrhistoricalwriting
@TraceyWarr1